professional
development

6. Creating a budget
and managing expenses
effectively

7. Investing in stocks,
real estate, or other
assets to build long-term
wealth

8. Balancing work and
life priorities to maintain
a healthy work-life
balance

9. Networking and
building relationships to
open up job

opportunities and
advance your career
10. Building a personal
brand and leveraging
social media to create
career opportunities

While there is no one-size-
fits-all approach to earning
money in your early 20s,
these topics could provide
useful guidance and insights
for young adults starting out
in the workforce. By
combining hard work,
ambition, and a strategic

approach, it is possible to achieve financial stability and set oneself up for long-term success.

1. Building a strong Financial foundations in your early 20s

Building a strong financial foundation in your early 20s is critical for achieving long-term financial stability and success. Here are some steps that can help you get started:

1.   Set financial goals: Define your financial goals, both short-term and long-term, and make a plan to achieve them. Whether you want to save for a down payment on a house, pay off your student loans, or start investing, having clear goals can help you stay motivated and focused.

2.   Create a budget: A budget is an essential tool for managing your

finances. Track your income and expenses, and identify areas where you can cut back on spending to save money. Make sure to include all of your expenses, such as rent, utilities, food, transportation, and entertainment.

3.   Save for emergencies: Building an emergency fund is crucial for handling unexpected expenses, such as medical bills or

car repairs. Aim to save at least three to six months' worth of living expenses in an easily accessible savings account.

4. Pay off debt: If you have student loans or credit card debt, make a plan to pay them off as soon as possible. Consider consolidating your debt or refinancing to lower your interest rates and reduce your monthly payments.

5.   Start investing: Investing early in life can help you build wealth over time. Consider investing in low-cost index funds or exchange-traded funds (ETFs) that track the performance of the stock market.

6.   Build your credit: Building good credit is essential for securing loans, renting an apartment, and even getting a job. Make sure

to pay your bills on time, keep your credit utilization low, and monitor your credit report regularly.

7.   Live within your means: Avoid the temptation to overspend and accumulate debt. Live below your means and make wise financial decisions that will set you up for long-term success.

By taking these steps, you can lay a strong foundation for your financial future in your early 20s. Remember, the key is to start early, be disciplined, and stay focused on your goals. With time and effort, you can achieve financial stability and security for the years to come.

2. Strategies for students to pay off student loan and managing debts

Student loans and other types of debt can be a significant burden for many young adults. Here are some strategies that can help you pay off your student loans and manage your debt effectively:

1.   Understand your loans: Make sure you understand the terms of your loans, including the interest rate, repayment period, and monthly payments. Keep track of your loans and make sure you are aware of any changes to your repayment terms.

2.   Create a repayment plan: Develop a repayment plan that works for your budget and financial goals.

Consider options such as the Standard Repayment Plan, the Graduated Repayment Plan, or the Income-Driven Repayment Plan. Use online calculators to compare your options and choose the best one for your situation.

3.   Pay more than the minimum: Whenever possible, try to pay more than the minimum required monthly payment. This will help

you pay off your loans faster and reduce the amount of interest you will pay over time.

4. Consolidate or refinance: Consider consolidating or refinancing your loans to lower your interest rates and reduce your monthly payments. Be sure to weigh the pros and cons of consolidation or refinancing, as there

may be trade-offs to consider.

5.   Prioritize your debts: If you have multiple types of debt, prioritize paying off the ones with the highest interest rates first. This will help you save money on interest over time and pay off your debts faster.

6.   Avoid late payments: Late payments can result in late fees, damage to your credit score, and even default on your

loans. Make sure to pay your bills on time and set up automatic payments if possible.

7.   Seek help if needed: If you are struggling to make your student loan payments or manage your debt, don't hesitate to seek help. Contact your loan servicer or a credit counseling agency to discuss your options.

By using these strategies, you can pay off your

student loans and manage your debt effectively. Remember, the key is to be proactive, stay organized, and stay committed to your financial goals. With time and effort, you can achieve financial freedom and security.

3. Identifying and pursuing career opportunities that align with your values and goals

Identifying and pursuing career opportunities that align with your values and goals is essential for achieving long-term career success and fulfillment. Here are some steps that can help you in this process:

1. Define your values and goals: Start by defining your personal values and career goals. Think about what motivates you and what you want to achieve in your career. Consider your passions, skills, and strengths, and how they can contribute to your success.

2.   Research career paths: Conduct research on different career paths that align with your values and goals. Use online resources such as job search websites, professional associations, and industry publications to learn about different career opportunities.

3.   Network: Networking is a critical tool for finding and pursuing career

opportunities. Attend industry events, join professional associations, and reach out to people in your network for advice and support.

4. Seek mentorship: Find a mentor who can guide you in your career development. Look for someone who has experience in your desired field and who shares your values and goals.

5.   Gain experience: Gain experience in your desired field through internships, volunteer work, or part-time jobs. This will help you build skills and knowledge and make you more attractive to potential employers.

6.   Evaluate job opportunities: Evaluate job opportunities based on how well they align with your values and goals. Consider factors

such as the company culture, job responsibilities, and potential for growth and development.

7.   Take calculated risks: Sometimes, taking calculated risks can lead to exciting career opportunities. Be willing to step out of your comfort zone and take on new challenges that can help you grow and develop.

By following these steps, you can identify and pursue career opportunities that align with your values and goals. Remember, the key is to stay focused, stay motivated, and stay committed to your career development. With time and effort, you can achieve the career success and fulfilment you desire.

4. Developing a side hustle or entrepreneurial venture to support your income

Developing a side hustle or entrepreneurial venture is a great way to supplement your income and achieve financial freedom. Here are some steps that can help you in this process:

1. Identify your skills and passions: Start by identifying your skills and passions. Think about what you enjoy doing and what skills you have that could be monetized.

2. Research potential business ideas: Conduct research on potential business ideas that align with your skills and passions. Look for gaps in the market and consider how you can

provide value to your customers.

3. Develop a business plan: Develop a business plan that outlines your goals, target market, marketing strategy, financial projections, and timeline. This will help you stay focused and organized as you launch your venture.

4. Build your brand: Build your brand by creating a website, social media presence,

and marketing materials that reflect your unique value proposition. This will help you attract customers and build credibility.

5.   Launch your venture: Launch your venture by testing your product or service in the market. Get feedback from customers and make adjustments as needed.

6.   Manage your finances: Manage your finances carefully by

setting a budget, tracking your expenses, and keeping accurate records. Consider using accounting software to make this process easier.

7.   Scale your venture: Once your venture is up and running, consider how you can scale it to increase your revenue and impact. This could include hiring employees, expanding your product line, or exploring new markets.

By following these steps, you can develop a side hustle or entrepreneurial venture that supplements your income and provides you with financial freedom. Remember, the key is to stay focused, stay motivated, and stay committed to your business goals. With time and effort, you can achieve the financial success and independence you desire.

5. Maximizing your earning potential through negotiation and professional development

Maximizing your earning potential involves a combination of negotiation skills and ongoing professional development.

Here are some tips on how to achieve both:

1.   Do your research: Before negotiating your salary or discussing career advancement with your employer, make sure you have a good understanding of industry standards and your own worth. Look at salary surveys, job postings, and other sources of information to get a sense of what

your skills and experience are worth in the market.

2.   Practice your negotiation skills: Negotiation is a skill that can be learned and practiced. Look for opportunities to negotiate in your personal life, such as when buying a car or negotiating rent with a landlord. This will help you build confidence

and develop your negotiation skills.

3.   Be prepared to make a case for yourself: When negotiating for a raise or promotion, be ready to explain why you deserve it. Highlight your accomplishments, skills, and contributions to the company. Make a clear case for why you should be paid more or given more responsibility.

4.   Keep learning and developing your skills: Continuous learning and development are essential for staying competitive in today's job market. Look for opportunities to improve your skills and knowledge, such as attending conferences, taking courses, or pursuing additional certifications.

5.   Seek out mentors and networking

opportunities: Mentors and networking can be valuable resources for career advice and opportunities. Look for people in your industry who you admire and respect and reach out to them for guidance and mentorship. Attend industry events and conferences to meet new people and expand your professional network.

By combining negotiation skills with ongoing professional development, you can maximize your earning potential and achieve your career goals. Remember to be confident, prepared, and always willing to learn and grow.

6. Creating a budget and managing expenses effectively

Creating a budget and managing expenses effectively is an essential part of financial planning. Here are some steps to help you create a budget and manage your expenses effectively:

1.   Determine your income: Start by calculating your total income for a given period, such as a month or a year. This includes any salaries, wages, bonuses, and other sources of income.

2.   List your expenses: Make a list of all your expenses for the same period, including fixed expenses like rent, utilities, and loan payments, as well as

variable expenses like food, entertainment, and transportation.

3. Categorize your expenses: Categorize your expenses into essential and non-essential expenses. Essential expenses are those that you must pay to live, while non-essential expenses are those that are discretionary.

4. Set priorities: Prioritize your expenses

and identify those that are most important. This will help you make informed decisions when you need to cut back on spending.

5.   Create a budget: Create a budget by allocating your income to your various expenses. Make sure to leave room for unexpected expenses and emergencies.

6.   Track your expenses: Keep track of your

expenses as you spend money. You can use a spreadsheet or a budgeting app to track your expenses.

7.   Review and adjust your budget: Review your budget regularly and make adjustments as necessary. This will help you stay on track and ensure that your budget reflects your changing financial situation.

Managing expenses effectively requires discipline and a willingness to make tough choices. By creating a budget and sticking to it, you can take control of your finances and achieve your financial goals. Remember to be flexible and adjust your budget as necessary to accommodate unexpected expenses and changes in your financial situation.

7.Investing in stocks, real estate or other assets to build long term wealth

Investing in stocks, real estate, or other assets is a great way to build long-term wealth. Here are some tips to help you get started:

1.   Determine your investment goals: Before investing, determine your investment goals. Do you want to invest for long-term growth or short-term gains? Are you looking for income or capital appreciation? Understanding your investment goals will help you make informed decisions about where to invest your money.

2.   Research potential investments: Research

potential investments
thoroughly before
investing. Look at
historical performance,
financial statements, and
other relevant
information. Consult
with financial advisors
and other professionals
to get expert advice.
3.   Diversify your
portfolio:
Diversification is key to
building a successful
investment portfolio.
Don't put all your money

in one investment or asset class. Instead, spread your investments across different types of assets, such as stocks, bonds, real estate, and commodities.

4.   Invest for the long-term: Investing for the long-term can help you weather short-term market fluctuations and maximize your returns. Avoid the temptation to make short-term trades based on market

fluctuations and focus on long-term investment strategies.

5.   Stay informed: Stay informed about market trends and changes that could impact your investments. Read financial news, follow industry experts, and stay up-to-date on economic indicators.

6.   Be patient and disciplined: Building long-term wealth through investing

requires patience and discipline. Stick to your investment plan, avoid emotional decisions based on short-term market fluctuations, and stay focused on your long-term goals.

Remember, investing always carries some risk. It's essential to do your research, understand your investment goals, and diversify your portfolio to minimize risk and maximize your returns. By following these tips and working with financial professionals when necessary, you can build long-term wealth through smart investing.

8.Balancing work and life priorities to maintain a healthy work-life balance

Maintaining a healthy work-life balance is essential to avoid burnout and live a fulfilling life. Here are some tips to help balance work and life priorities:

1. Set boundaries: Establish clear boundaries between work and personal time. Avoid checking work emails or taking work calls outside of work hours, and try to disconnect from work when you're not at work.

2. Prioritize self-care: Take care of yourself both physically and mentally. Get enough sleep, exercise regularly, and eat a healthy diet.

Take time for relaxation and hobbies that bring you joy.

3. Learn to say no: Don't overcommit yourself. Learn to say no to requests that would take up too much time or energy.

4. Manage your time effectively: Manage your time effectively by setting priorities and using tools like calendars and to-do lists. Schedule time for work

tasks, personal tasks, and leisure activities.

5. Communicate with your employer: Communicate with your employer about your need for work-life balance. Discuss options like flexible scheduling, telecommuting, or reduced work hours.

6. Avoid multitasking: Multitasking can lead to decreased productivity and increased stress. Focus on one task at a

time and avoid
distractions.

7.   Spend quality time
with loved ones: Make
time for family and
friends. Plan activities
that you enjoy together
and make the most of
the time you have
together.

Remember that achieving
work-life balance is an
ongoing process that
requires constant attention
and adjustment. By setting

boundaries, prioritizing self-care, managing your time effectively, communicating with your employer, avoiding multitasking, and spending quality time with loved ones, you can achieve a healthy work-life balance and live a fulfilling life.

9.Networking and building relationship to open up job opportunities and advance your carrier

Networking and building relationships is a crucial element in opening up job opportunities and advancing your career. Here are some steps that can help you in this process:

1. Identify your networking goals: Start by identifying your networking goals. Consider what type of job opportunities you are looking for and the type of people you need to connect with to achieve those goals.

2.   Build your network:
Build your network by
attending industry
events, joining
professional
associations, and
connecting with people
in your field. Use online
tools such as LinkedIn
to connect with potential
contacts.

3.   Establish a rapport:
Establish a rapport with
your network by
showing genuine interest
in their work and

accomplishments. Ask questions, listen actively, and look for opportunities to help them achieve their goals.

4.   Follow up: Follow up with your contacts regularly to maintain your relationships. Send them articles or information that may be of interest to them, invite them to events, and offer to introduce them to other contacts in your network.

5.   Offer value: Offer value to your contacts by sharing your expertise, introducing them to potential clients or job opportunities, or providing them with resources that can help them achieve their goals.

6.   Be authentic: Be authentic and genuine in your interactions with your contacts. People can tell when you are not being sincere, so it is important to be yourself

and build relationships based on trust and mutual respect.

7.   Be patient: Building a strong network takes time and patience. Don't expect immediate results, and don't be discouraged if you don't see immediate job opportunities. Focus on building strong relationships, and the opportunities will come.

By following these steps, you can build a strong network and open up job opportunities and advance your career. Remember, the key is to stay focused, stay motivated, and stay committed to your networking goals. With time and effort, you can achieve the career success and fulfilment you desire.

10.Building a personal brand and leveraging social media to create career opportunities

Building a personal brand and leveraging social media is a powerful way to create career opportunities and establish yourself as a thought leader in your field.

Here are some steps that can help you in this process:

1. Define your personal brand: Start by defining your personal brand. Consider your unique skills, values, and experiences, and how you want to be perceived by others in your field.

2. Create a professional online presence: Create a professional online presence by establishing

profiles on LinkedIn, Twitter, and other social media platforms that are relevant to your field.

3.   Develop content: Develop content that showcases your expertise and thought leadership. This can include blog posts, articles, videos, podcasts, and social media updates.

4.   Share your content: Share your content on social media and other

relevant platforms to increase your visibility and reach. Engage with your audience and respond to comments and questions to build relationships.

5. Network with influencers: Network with influencers in your field by commenting on their posts, sharing their content, and attending events where they will be speaking.

6. Collaborate with others: Collaborate with other professionals in your field to increase your exposure and reach. This can include guest blogging, co-hosting a podcast, or participating in a panel discussion.

7. Be consistent: Consistency is key when building a personal brand. Stay focused on your goals, share valuable content on a

regular basis, and engage with your audience consistently to build trust and credibility.

By following these steps, you can build a strong personal brand and leverage social media to create career opportunities. Remember, the key is to stay focused, stay motivated, and stay committed to your personal brand goals. With time and effort, you can achieve the

career success and
recognition you desire.

Thanking you.....

The end.....